HOUGHTON MIFFLIN HARCOURT

Respect and Protect

Welcome, Reader!

In this magazine you will explore places from the Milky Way to Death Valley, from the Alaska Range to the African savannah. You'll investigate animals as big as a colossal squid and as small as a honeybee.

You'll read poems and articles about wild storms and outer space, and interact with nature through lots of fun activities.

Your adventure begins as soon as you turn the page!

English-Language Arts Content Standards for California Public Schools reproduced by permission, California Department of Education, CDE Press, 1430 N Street, Suite 3207, Sacramento, CA 95814.

"Moon" from *Space Songs* by Myra Cohn Livingston. Text copyright © 1988 by Myra Cohn Livingston. Reprinted by permission of the author c/o Marian Reiner, Literary Agent. "Satellites" from *Space Songs* by Myra Cohn Livingston. Text copyright © 1988 by Myra Cohn Livingston. Reprinted by permission of the author c/o Marian Reiner, Literary Agent. "Twelve Below" from *Letters from Maine* by May Sarton. Copyright © 1984 by May Sarton. Reprinted by permission of W. W. Norton & Co. "Desert Day" from *Central Heating: Poems About Fire and Warmth* by Marilyn Singer. Text copyright © 2005 by Marilyn Singer. Reprinted by permission of Alfred A. Knopf, an imprint of Random House Children's Books, a division of Random House, Inc. "Straight Talk" by Nikki Grimes. Copyright © by Nikki Grimes. Reprinted by permission of Curtis Brown Ltd. "An evenly balanced word W H A L E..." from *Words with Wrinkled Knees: Animal Poems* by Barbara Juster Esbensen. Text copyright © 1986 by Barbara Juster Esbensen. Reprinted by permission of Wordsong, a division of Boyds Mills Press, Inc. "Snow" from *A Pocketful of Poems* by Nikki Grimes. Text copyright © 2001 by Nikki Grimes. Reprinted by permission of Houghton Mifflin Harcourt Publishing Company. "The Elephant" by Hilaire Belloc. Reprinted by permission of Gerard Duckworth and Co. Ltd. "The Wind" from *Mummy Took Cooking Lessons and Other Poems* by John Ciardi. Text copyright © 1990 by Judith C. Ciardi. Reprinted by permission of Houghton Mifflin Harcourt Publishing Company.

Printed in the U.S.A.

ISBN-13: 978-0-547-07392-7

4 5 6 7 8 9 0914 14 13 12 11 10 09

Respect and Protect

SPACE

Oxygen pack. *Check*. Tether cord. *Check*. Cameras. *Check*. Thermal gloves. *Check*. Astronaut Ed White was ready.

Boosting himself out of the *Gemini 4* hatch, White began America's first space walk. It was 1965. White beamed as he floated at the end of his twenty-five-foot tether, shooting photographs. Too soon, the spectacular walk ended. White made his way slowly back to the spacecraft. But before he handed his gear to his fellow astronaut, he dropped a spare glove! That glove joined an assortment of odds and ends we call space trash.

Over the years, the trash circling around our globe has grown. Space shuttle *Atlantis* astronauts lost a couple of bolts in space. *Discovery* astronauts lost a spatula while repairing their shuttle with special putty. A camera, bits of broken equipment, and even garbage bags tossed out by the Mir space station have added to the debris in space. At least 10,000 pieces of junk measuring four inches or larger are orbiting our planet. The United States space program tracks this trash because even though the debris is way up in space, it could cause us big problems here on earth if it hits something.

TRASH

IT STARTED WITH THE SATELLITES

For fifty years now, people have been sending objects into space. Some of those things have been brought safely down to earth, but others have been left in space to drift.

It all began in 1957, when the Soviet Union launched *Sputnik 1*, the world's first artificial satellite. A satellite is anything that revolves around a planet and is held in orbit by the gravitational pull of the planet. Our moon, for instance, is a natural satellite. Artificial satellites are objects that people make and send into space.

To launch satellites out of earth's atmosphere and into space, rockets must travel at least 18,000 miles per hour and fly more than 120 miles into the sky. Such rockets have several powerful engines, a large supply of fuel, and a *payload*. The payload is the object being sent into the sky, like a satellite. When the rocket fires its engines one after another, the used-up parts of the rocket fall away and become part of space trash.

Sputnik 1 circled the earth every 96 minutes. The United States launched its first satellite, *Explorer 1*, the next year. Scientists used *Explorer 1* to measure how much radiation earth had in its atmosphere. Today, about 850 satellites orbit our planet.

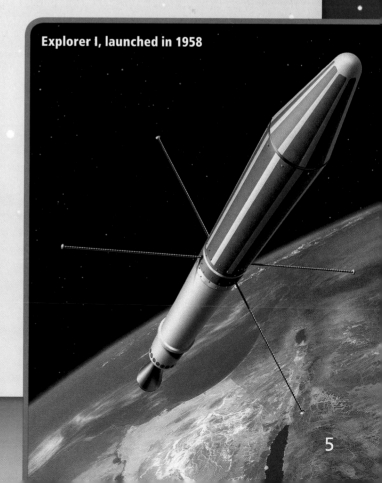

Explorer I, launched in 1958

5

We use satellites every day. When you send a text message or use your cell phone to make a call, a satellite in space sends and receives your messages.

Satellites also bring television programs from all over the world to people's homes. They send meteorologists (scientists who study the weather) pictures of cloud formations from high above so that the meteorologist on the morning news can tell us whether to bundle up for snow or to grab an umbrella for rain. Some car passengers use satellites about 12,000 miles above us to track where they are on a digital map located on the car dashboard.

When satellites are no longer useful, they become part of the ring of space trash around the earth. They circle the globe with the pieces of the rocket that first brought them up into space.

The Corot, a French satellite, shown here in computer art, was launched in 2006 to study stars and search for distant planets.

IN AND OUT OF ORBIT

Around our planet lies a 60-mile-thick blanket of air called our atmosphere. The farther from earth, the thinner the air becomes. Gravity also becomes weaker. Satellites and space trash orbit outside earth's atmosphere and remain in orbit because of their speed, or velocity. Earth's gravity holds such objects just enough to keep them from flying off into outer space.

After many, many orbits, a satellite begins to lose velocity. Gravity wins the battle and pulls the object downward. It then drops to earth at an extremely fast speed. This speed creates intense heat that makes the object burn. Spacecraft also heat up when they enter the atmosphere on a trip back to earth.

Russian space experts think *Sputnik I* and the *Sputnik* satellites that followed burned up this way. But the people of Manitowoc, Wisconsin, see things differently. They believe that *Sputnik IV* landed in their town in 1962, right in the middle of Eighth Street. A big chunk of metal lay embedded into the middle of the street, while two police officers puzzled over it. Finally, the townspeople sent the 20-pound lump of metal to Washington, D.C. From there, it was returned to the Soviet Union. Today, a brass ring marks the spot on the street in Manitowoc where the chunk landed.

The incident in Wisconsin wasn't the only time space trash has fallen into an area where people live. In 1997, a 500-pound rocket fuel tank landed in a field close to a Texas farmhouse. In 2000, people in South Africa found a large, battered metal tank in a dusty field. Though it looked like a giant ostrich egg, it was a piece of space trash that had fallen to earth.

This chunk of space metal smashed the roof of a house in Oberhausen, Germany in 1999.

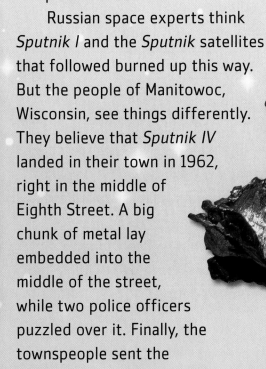

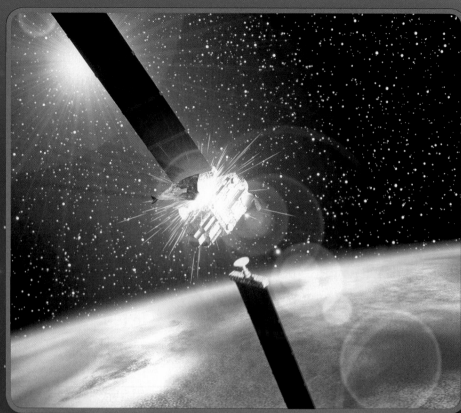

In this artist's simulation, a sliver of metal collides with a satellite's solar panel.

WHY WORRY?

While most objects that reenter the earth's atmosphere burn up, scientists agree that some space trash can survive the fall to earth. Most of this junk they expect to fall into areas with few or no people, such as the world's vast ocean, desert, or tundra areas.

Even though it's extremely unlikely that falling space trash will harm anyone, there's a good reason to worry about space trash. This junk can hit other spacecraft.

An object must travel 17,000 miles per hour to stay in orbit. An object the size of a tennis ball traveling at that speed could seriously damage weather satellites, space telescopes, and other instruments used for gathering information.

Even things as small as chips of paint could damage other objects at such high speeds. A chip of paint made a nick in a window of the space shuttle *Challenger*. Scientists believe the dangers of this whirling junk belt around our planet will continue to grow, as objects continue colliding and creating more debris.

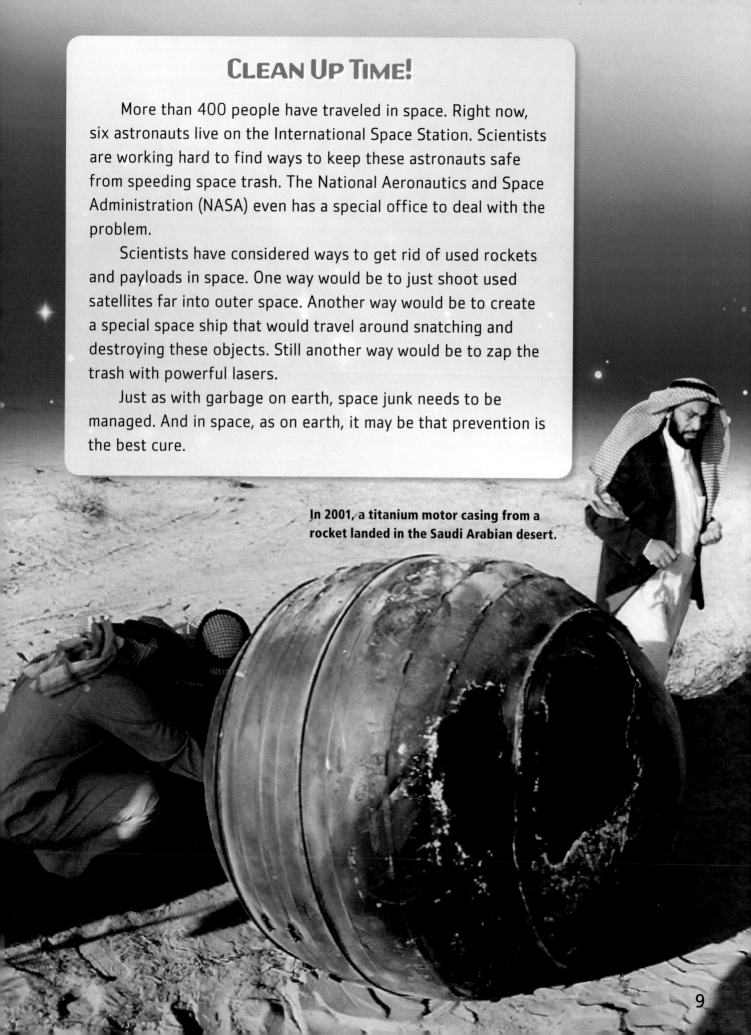

CLEAN UP TIME!

More than 400 people have traveled in space. Right now, six astronauts live on the International Space Station. Scientists are working hard to find ways to keep these astronauts safe from speeding space trash. The National Aeronautics and Space Administration (NASA) even has a special office to deal with the problem.

Scientists have considered ways to get rid of used rockets and payloads in space. One way would be to just shoot used satellites far into outer space. Another way would be to create a special space ship that would travel around snatching and destroying these objects. Still another way would be to zap the trash with powerful lasers.

Just as with garbage on earth, space junk needs to be managed. And in space, as on earth, it may be that prevention is the best cure.

In 2001, a titanium motor casing from a rocket landed in the Saudi Arabian desert.

How the Milky Way

Long ago, when time began, there were only a few stars in the sky. When people looked up at night, the sky was almost completely black.

At that time people depended on corn for their food. They would dry some of the corn and grind it into cornmeal. They stored the cornmeal outside in large baskets. During the cold winters, people would use cornmeal to make delicious corn bread and mush.

One morning when an elderly couple went to fetch some cornmeal, they found their basket overturned. Cornmeal was scattered all over the ground. The couple was upset. Stealing was unheard of in Cherokee villages. Who could have done such a thing?

As they looked more closely at the ground, they noticed what looked like a dog's paw prints. But these paw prints were huge. No dog they had ever seen was that size.

The couple went quickly to tell the other villagers about what had happened. After hearing the story, the people decided the dog must have been a spirit dog. They didn't want the dog coming back to their village, so they made a plan.

Came To Be
A Cherokee Tale:

When the dog returned, they would frighten it away. That night, people collected all their drums and rattles and hid behind the cornmeal basket, waiting.

Suddenly they heard what sounded like a flock of birds with their wings all flapping at once. A doglike shape came down from the sky. It landed near the cornmeal basket. The dog stuck its nose inside and began to eat the cornmeal.

Jumping out from behind the basket, the villagers banged their drums and shook their rattles. They made the biggest racket they could. The frightened dog ran from the village with the people chasing it. It ran to the top of a hill and leaped into the sky, the cornmeal falling from its mouth.

The dog ran across the black sky until it was out of sight. The cornmeal that had fallen from its mouth made a pattern of stars. The Cherokee call this pattern of stars *Gil'liutsun stanun' yi*, which means "the place where the dog ran."

And that's the story of how the Milky Way came to be.

11

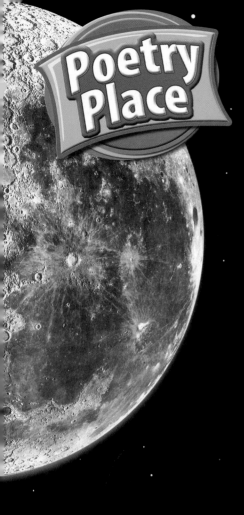

MOON

By Myra Cohn Livingston

Moon remembers.

Marooned in shadowed night,

white powder plastered
on her pockmarked face,
scarred with craters,
filled with waterless seas,
she thinks back
to the Eagle,
to the flight
of men from Earth,
of rocks sent back in space,
and one
faint
footprint
in the Sea of Tranquility.

Monitors of steel,
these space detectives seek
clues to the beginning of our galaxy.
Informers of the energy of stars, of gamma rays;
weighted with sensors,
They listen, watch, and speak
of radiation, solar flares,
atmospheric density.
Stalking magnetic fields,
they serve out their days.

SATELLITES

By Myra Cohn Livingston

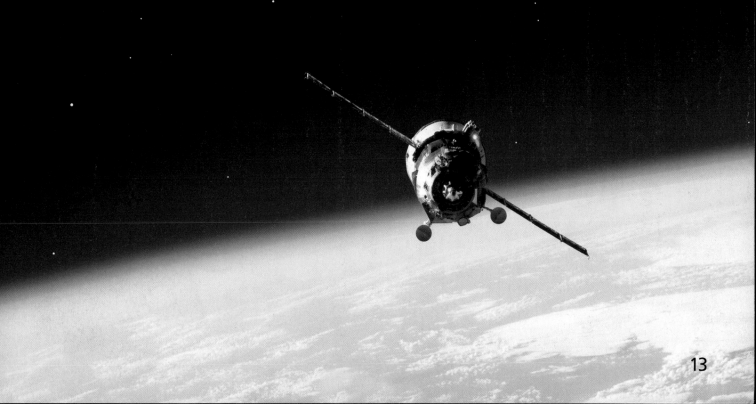

SPACE!

Imagine you are a board game manufacturer. Working with a partner, or in small group, create a game in which the goal is to clean up the debris floating around in space. Write a set of rules and instructions that make it clear how the game is played and how it's won. Include a set of "chance" cards to make the game more interesting. After you've created the instructions, design the board. Once your game is complete, swap with other groups and play.

Some say sun,

Some say star.

sunshine sunshine sunshine sunshine sunshine sunshine

Either way,

it shines from afar.

Look Up!
Shape Poems

You've
just read two
poems that take the shape
of their subject. Now try writing
your own shape poem. All you need is
a pencil and some paper. First pick something that would appear in the sky—a star,
the sun, a planet, a rocket, or a comet, for
example. Next, write a short poem about that
object, not worrying yet about the shape.
Once you've written the poem the way
you want it, draw the shape of the
poem on a piece of paper. Then
write the words into the
shape.

Catch that Trash!

In "Space Trash," you learned about the thousands of pieces of space debris and the dangers they pose. How do we get rid of this trash? Design a device to clean up space trash. Imagine that you're applying for a patent for your invention. Draw a picture of the trash picker, label its parts, and write a statement explaining how it works.

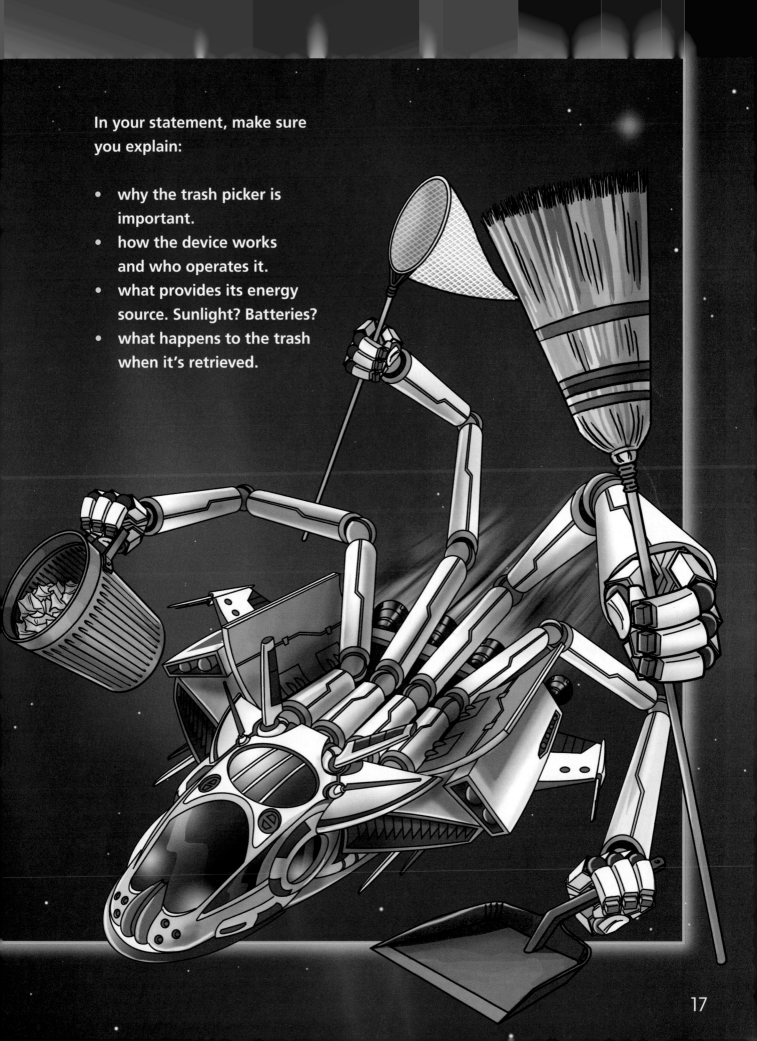

In your statement, make sure you explain:

- why the trash picker is important.
- how the device works and who operates it.
- what provides its energy source. Sunlight? Batteries?
- what happens to the trash when it's retrieved.

Denali Dog Sled Journal

Saturday, December 8:

Today is Saturday, but we Denali National Park rangers have to patrol our part of the park's six million acres every day, so I climbed onto the sled runners and my dog team took off.

We have a week-long patrol ahead of us. The dogs looked as excited as I feel when I start on patrol. The dog team patrols started in the 1920s, soon after Denali became Alaska's first park. We can't take cars or snowmobiles into the park, so the dogs pulling the sleds are our transportation. The dogs allow us to take care of visitors, haul supplies, and watch to be sure all is well. We glide over the snow-covered ground. The ground under the snow is called permafrost. It stays frozen throughout the year.

Sled dogs, also known as Alaskan huskies, are strong runners. They have two layers of thick fur to keep them warm, and they follow orders well.

Dog team at Wonder Lake

We were lucky today because there had been no snowstorm. The trail was clear. We easily traveled the thirty miles to the first patrol cabin. I was glad to get a fire going and heat up soup. My traveling companions were tail-wagging happy to see full dog food bowls!

Sunday, December 9:

A snowstorm kicked up during the night. All day today I walked ahead of the team to clear the trail. As I shoveled snow out of the way, I uncovered a small bush. I marvel at the plants that manage to survive these frigid temperatures.

While there are only eight types of trees in Denali National Park, there are many types of shrubs, like alders. Alders thrive in ground that has been disturbed by rockslides. Hundreds of other plants survive the winters, including wild-flowers such as fireweed.

As I cleared the trail, a wolf howled in the distance, and the dogs howled back.

Fireweed in the snow

Thirty-nine types of mammals in the park also manage to survive the cold. Mice tunnel under the snow where they can stay warmer. Moose, caribou, and sheep search for food all winter. Grizzly bears hibernate. A long snooze sounds good to me, too!

Dinosaurs once roamed the Denali National Park area. In 2005, dinosaur footprints were found in the park.

Monday, December 10:

When I radioed in my report to park headquarters, I learned there was an earthquake early this morning. As with most of our earthquakes, I never even noticed it. The quakes are the result of the Denali Fault which cuts through the park.

The Denali is North America's largest fault. On either side of this deep crack, the plates of Earth's crust move a tiny bit all the time. Over millions of years, the plates shaped the 600-mile sweep of mountains called the Alaska Range.

Today in the patrol cabin, I had a chess partner! No, I haven't taught one of the dogs the game. My partner was Dr. Chang, a scientist who is studying the park's winter wildlife. The dogs and I bring him supplies. In return, he feeds us stew and popcorn, and we share his cozy fire.

Avalanche from a Denali quake

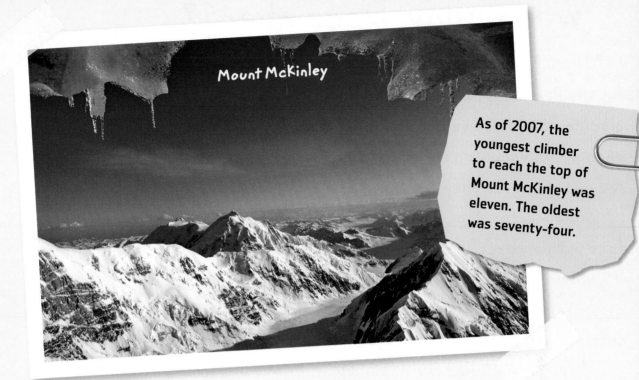

Mount McKinley

As of 2007, the youngest climber to reach the top of Mount McKinley was eleven. The oldest was seventy-four.

Tuesday, December 11:

As I left Dr. Chang's cabin today, I received a radio call. Two snowshoers, Andy and Marla Perez, had not checked in at the Wilderness Access Center. I passed Wonder Lake, where visitors often go for the view of Mount McKinley. At 20,320 feet it is North America's tallest mountain. Native Americans called it *Denali*, which means "the high one."

People have climbed Mount McKinley since 1910. Every year, between May and the first week in July, more than one thousand people try to reach the top of the mountain. About one of every two climbers reaches the top.

There was no sign of the Perezes, so the dogs and I moved on toward the patrol cabin. I saw moose tracks, but no snow-shoe tracks. At the cabin, I talked to headquarters. There had been no word from Andy and Marla Perez. Tonight we are all worried about them. Where are they? Are they okay?

Wednesday, December 12:

This morning I traveled to Muldrow Glacier, searching for the Perezes. I only hoped the Perezes hadn't hiked on a glacier. Glaciers have cracks called crevasses that can be big enough to swallow an entire dog sled. Crevasses are hard to see under snow so they are very dangerous.

Suddenly the dogs yipped and growled. We were face to face with a moose! He didn't look glad to see us—in fact, he looked angry. I quickly turned the dogs around. We zoomed off across a frozen river. I could see a small cabin on the far shore. I headed toward it.

As we approached the cabin, I was surprised to see a kerosene lamp glowing through the window. Even better were the two sets of snowshoes next to the door. The Perezes were as excited to see me as I was to see them! They had gotten lost and weren't able to make their way back to the Wilderness Access Center. They were lucky to find the cabin.

A glacier is made when snow falls over many years and turns into ice. A glacier flows very slowly, like a river in slow motion.

Maldrow Glacier

Bull moose on a ridge

It was a treat to share our stories. It gets lonely out on patrol. Andy and Marla gladly agreed to my offer of a ride in my dog sled for the next two days. They were tired from all that snowshoeing. As I write this, they're playing with the dogs, who enjoy company as much as I do.

Thursday, December 13:

Marla and Andy and I talked about how little Denali National Park has changed over the years. Traveling through it by dog sled feels the way it must have felt in the old days, complete with the dangers and pleasures. Sled dog travel maintains a tradition important to the park.

The Perezes were amazed when I told them the south side of the park is completely different from the north. It's a panorama of lofty, sharp mountain peaks and dark, thick forests. I told them they should fly over it. Flying is the best way to see the area, which is too densely wooded to travel by foot.

The park kennels

Friday, December 14:

Marla and Andy are on their way home, but they say they will be back to visit.

I spent the morning doing paperwork. In the afternoon, I gave my report to the ranger who will cover my area next. Before I headed home, I visited the dogs' kennels. I patted each of the dogs I'd just spent a week with, thanking them for taking such good care of me.

I have a few days off now. All the better to rest up for my next adventures on sled dog patrol!

Native Athabaskans have lived in the Denali area for about eleven thousand years. They lived off the land, eating game, berries, and fish. When winter came, they sheltered in low valleys.

Today, many Athabaskans still depend on the land's bounty. They grow gardens and pick berries, hunt and fish, and harvest wood for fuel and building material.

Denali National Park

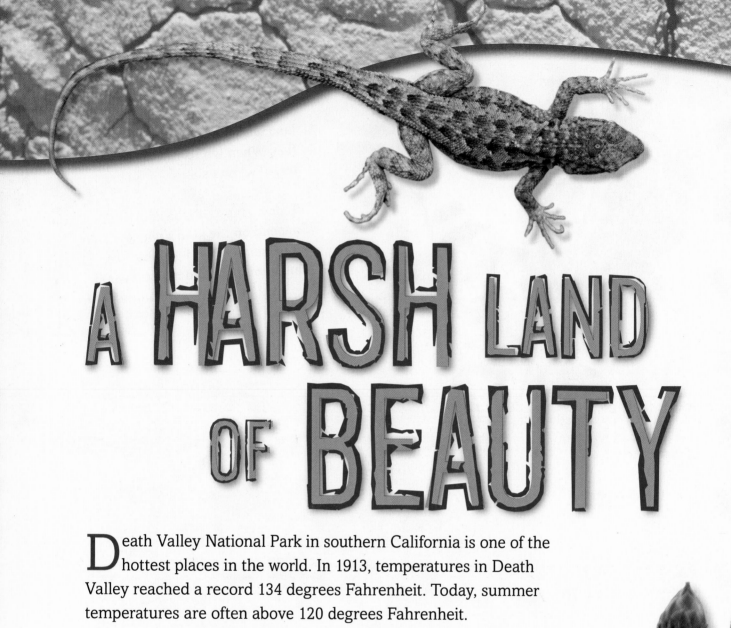

A HARSH LAND OF BEAUTY

Death Valley National Park in southern California is one of the hottest places in the world. In 1913, temperatures in Death Valley reached a record 134 degrees Fahrenheit. Today, summer temperatures are often above 120 degrees Fahrenheit.

The shape of the valley contributes to its hot, dry weather. High mountains surround the valley and act like walls to hold in the heat. The heat evaporates water quickly, making the air and soil very dry. The valley once held a lake, but the water evaporated over time, leaving behind a thick crust of salt. Within this salty area is the lowest point in North America.

Plants and animals have different adaptations for surviving in this harsh environment. Some plants have long roots that reach down more than ten times the height of a person in search of water. Other plants have shallow roots that reach in many directions to gather water quickly after winter rains. Most plants have thick stems and leaves that prevent water from evaporating. Many animals survive the heat by being active at night and hiding under rocks and in burrows during the day.

In 1849, a group of pioneers barely survived their journey across what is now Death Valley. The pioneers thought the valley was a shortcut to California, where they hoped to make their fortunes panning for gold. They faced water shortages and great hardship as they traveled. Afterwards, the region was named Death Valley.

TWELVE BELOW

By May Sarton

A bitter gale
Over frozen snow
Burns the skin like hail.
It is twelve below.

Too cold to live
Too cold to die
Warm animals wait
And make no cry.

Their feathers puff
Their eyes are bright
Their fur expands.
Warm animals wait.

They make no sign
They waste no breath
In this cold country
Between life and death.

DESERT DAY

By Marilyn Singer

Denizens of the desert
 understand under, inside,
 between, below.
Each rattlesnake, wren,
 rabbit, fox, or spider
lays claim to every scrubby tree and cactus,
 arroyo, burrow, boulder, branch
to sleep, or sit out the sun.
And when moving is a must,
 they wheel, flap, sidewind, scuttle,
 run across the blistering sand.
Denizens of the desert
 learn to balance
 the stillness and the scramble.
Few amble.

Extreme Museum

Hottest and coldest. Wettest and driest. Highest and lowest. These are examples of extremes.

You've just been hired as a member of a team in charge of a new museum called the Extreme Museum. You must decide on what extremes to exhibit. Working in small groups or pairs, follow the steps below to get your museum ready for its grand opening.

1. **Plan your museum.** Make a list of as many extremes as you can think of. Each member of your team should then choose one set of extremes to put on display.

2. **Find your objects.** Cut up old magazines or print out pictures from a computer. For example, if your extremes are most furry and least furry, you might look for pictures of a sheepdog and a hairless cat.

3. **Display your collection.** Glue your pictures to a piece of cardboard. Write a sentence explaining the pairs. Prop up or hang your extremes around your classroom.

most furry

least furry

Letter Play

An anagram is a word or phrase formed by rearranging the letters of another word or phrase. Rearrange the following anagrams to find some words that you read in "Denali Dog Sled Journal." Use the clue below the anagram if you need help with the answer.

Example

county milkmen
Clue: highest mountain in North America
answer: Mount McKinley

Anagrams

1. **ace girl**
   Clue: slow-moving river of ice

2. **lasagna rake**
   Clue: 600 miles of mountains in Denali

3. **nailed**
   Clue: "the high one" in Athabaskan

4. **whose sons**
   Clue: used to walk on snow without sinking

5. **farmer spot**
   Clue: layer of soil and ice that is always frozen

6. **a snake hauls ski**
   Clue: another term for *sled dogs*

7. **a keen world**
   Clue: body of water with a wonderful view

8. **log paddles rot**
   Clue: team of huskies on the job

Answers
1. glacier • 2. Alaska range • 3. Denali • 4. snowshoes • 5. permafrost • 6. Alaska huskies • 7. Wonder Lake • 8. sled dog patrol

Stay

What does it take to survive the frozen tundra or a hot desert? Animals and plants have special adaptations that allow them to survive in harsh environments. But how do people deal with extreme cold or heat? Working with a partner or in small groups, imagine you've been chosen to write a survival guide for a research team going to a very hot or a very cold place for a month. Your guide will help the team survive—whether it's Antarctica or the Sahara Desert.

Alive!

First, research your destination. Gather information on its climate, vegetation, and animal life. Next, create a section in your guide for each of these areas. Be sure to note what kind of clothing is necessary, where to find food, and the dangers that nature may pose. Finally, summarize the most important points for survival.

Vanishing Act

Thousands more like this one are missing in action.

It's a mystery. Call me.

The morning the dead bee arrived in the mail, my mind was already buzzing with ideas. Unfortunately, none of them were about my science project. The letter addressed to me had grabbed my attention.

"A note from my cousin Justin," I thought at first. I nearly tossed the envelope aside, but Justin's handwriting, was usually close to impossible to read.

This was unusually careful and clear. I opened the envelope and unfolded the piece of blue paper inside. A bee carcass fell on my desk.

At least I thought it was a bee. I always have a hard time telling apart flying, stinging insects–such as wasps, hornets, and bees–when they're alive. A dead one was even trickier to identify. The note said:

"Thousands more like this one are missing in action. It's a mystery. Call me."

No signature on the note. But it was from Justin. I was sure of it.

I found a magnifying glass and studied the dead bug my cousin had sent. I compared it to images in the encyclopedia. I learned that wasps always have yellow and black stripes, whereas honeybees are often a golden brown. Since bees in cartoons are almost always yellow-and-black striped and cute, you can understand my initial confusion. But the dead insect was definitely a honeybee. I picked up the phone to call Justin.

"Hey, stop sending dead stuff to me," I said when he picked up.

"It got your attention, didn't it?" he replied.

"What's going on?" I asked.

"I'm at Grandpa Ray's farm. When we got here on Friday night, he was having a fit because the hives he rented were empty," Justin said.

"Wait a second. Your grandpa rents hives?" I asked. Justin's Grandpa Ray wasn't my grandpa but I'd been to his farm dozens of times. I'd learned a lot about farming from the visits, but I had no idea what Justin was talking about. "Empty hives?"

"Yeah, lots of farmers rent beehives," Justin said, clearly impatient with me. "Grandpa has beekeepers bring hives here every February for the almond harvest. All the farmers do it. Grandpa said they need millions of bees to pollinate the crops. And that's just for the almond orchards."

Raising bees was a much bigger business than I'd imagined. Our class went on a field trip to visit beekeepers when we were in fourth grade. We learned all about pollination from a beekeeper who wore what looked like a white space suit that completely covered her.

The insect carcass fell out of the envelope. On close inspection, I determined it was, indeed, a dead honeybee.

35

I was mostly interested in the beeswax candles and jars of honey that they sold in the gift shop, so I kind of forgot that bees have a bigger job in the scheme of things. If honeybees don't pollinate plants, those plants won't reproduce and make seeds for new plants. Farmers could get desperate for bees.

"I need you to come out here and take a look. I need you to be my eyes," Justin said.

"What *I* need to do is to come up with an idea for a science project. And it can't be just one of my regular kind of brilliant ideas. This has to be *especially* brilliant because the whole town will see it at the science fair. If I don't have something by dinner, Mom will ground me and I'll never get to see you again," I said.

"Tia," Justin said with a long, dramatic sigh. "Don't you get it? This *is* your science project. That's why I wrote to you."

"What about my keen observational skills?" I asked.

"That too."

Justin was a year ahead of me in school and he knew all about the required seventh-grade independent scence project. He was right. An investigation into the missing honeybees *did* sound like a good science project.

I'd seen a beekeeper in full protective gear.

36

When Mom got back from the store, we decided to take a trip to the farm. I called Justin and arranged to meet him there in the afternoon.

When we arrived at the farm, Mom went into the house to visit Grandma Ray. Grandpa Ray took Justin and me out to the orchards, narrating our walk as if we were being filmed for a TV nature television program. "Bees pollinate more than 90 crops in the U.S. We bring them in every spring for the almonds. We use them for avocadoes, cherries, and kiwis, too. But look what we have here." He stopped at a hive, poking it with a stick. "Go ahead and look. Believe me, nothing will hurt you."

I peered inside.

"It's empty," I said, taking a photograph.

"Exactly," Grandpa Ray said.

Would someone steal them and then sell them or rent them to another farmer?" I asked.

"Seems like they'd need to take the whole hive in order to make any money," Justin commented.

"I'm afraid some young yahoo is trying to cause trouble. Probably doesn't realize that without bees there won't be as much food," Grandpa Ray said. "So much of what we eat wouldn't be possible without honeybees. In California, the almond crops alone are worth about two billion dollars."

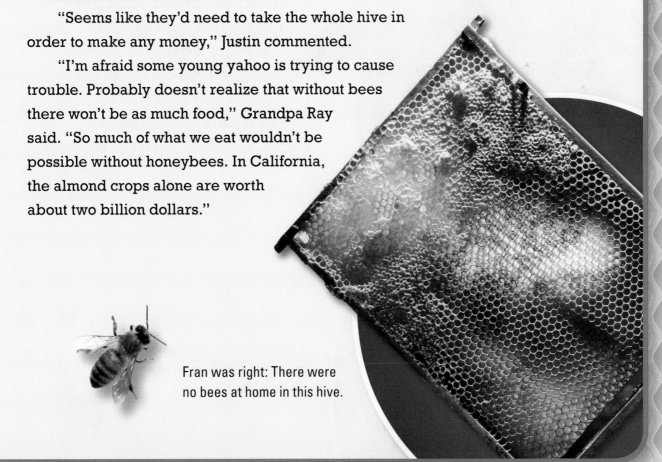

Fran was right: There were no bees at home in this hive.

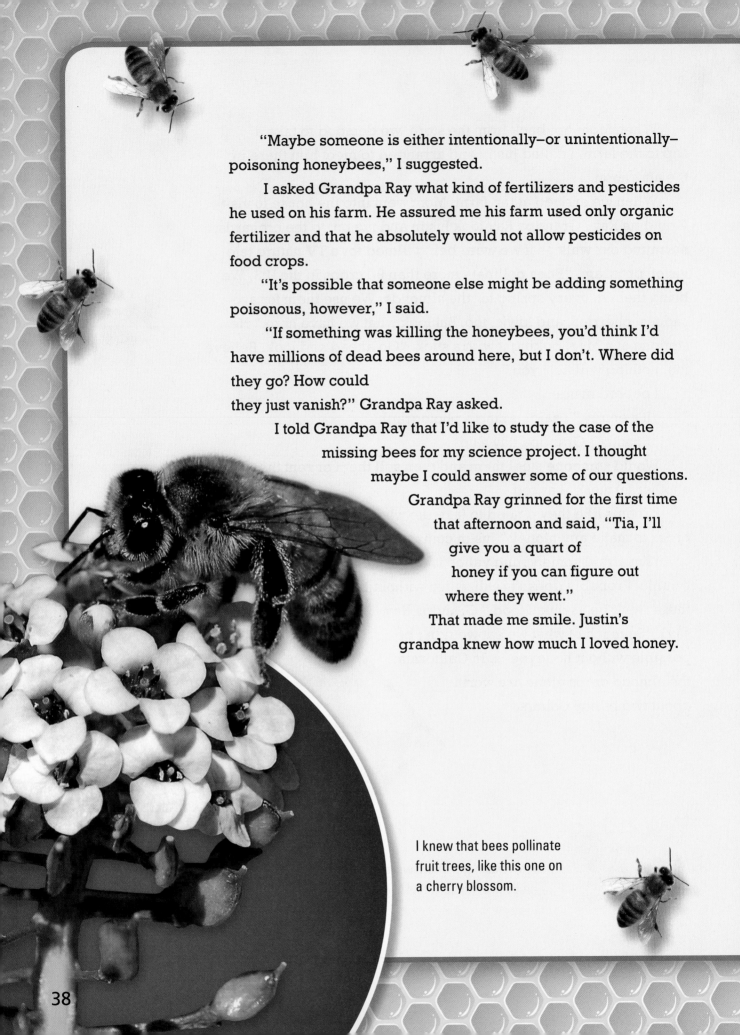

"Maybe someone is either intentionally—or unintentionally—poisoning honeybees," I suggested.

I asked Grandpa Ray what kind of fertilizers and pesticides he used on his farm. He assured me his farm used only organic fertilizer and that he absolutely would not allow pesticides on food crops.

"It's possible that someone else might be adding something poisonous, however," I said.

"If something was killing the honeybees, you'd think I'd have millions of dead bees around here, but I don't. Where did they go? How could they just vanish?" Grandpa Ray asked.

I told Grandpa Ray that I'd like to study the case of the missing bees for my science project. I thought maybe I could answer some of our questions.

Grandpa Ray grinned for the first time that afternoon and said, "Tia, I'll give you a quart of honey if you can figure out where they went."

That made me smile. Justin's grandpa knew how much I loved honey.

I knew that bees pollinate fruit trees, like this one on a cherry blossom.

I started on my project right away and began by taking several dozen photographs around the farm as well as the surrounding landscape.

Was it crazy to think someone would intentionally steal or kill honeybees?

When we got back to the farmhouse, I hooked my camera up to Justin's laptop so I could look at the photos I'd taken.

"Tell me what you see there," Justin said, moving his head so he could see from the corner of his eye. Justin's legally blind, but that doesn't mean he's totally blind. He has peripheral vision, which means he can see things off to the side. It takes people a while to get used to how he moves so that he can see their faces. He uses a computer all the time, but it would be next to impossible for him to see any details that would be in the photographs that I just took. I zoomed in on one photo.

"What do you see?" Justin asked, leaning in.

"It's what I don't see," I said. "It looks like a large electricity transmitter, but there aren't any wires going into it or coming out of it."

"Sounds like a cell site," Justin said.

"A sell sight?" I asked. "What's that?"

"For cell phones. They pick up cell phone signals." Justin launched into a long description of how my cell phone worked. My mind was elsewhere.

Could this be a clue?

Justin knew it was a cell site in my photo. Could cell phone signals interfere with honeybees?

Almond orchards in California produce a harvest worth two billion dollars each year.

When we got home, I told Mom I was off to research the disappearance of the honeybees. In just a couple of hours of online research I'd learned that our county wasn't the only one with missing honeybees. Since the fall of 2006, more than twenty-five states reported dramatic declines in the number of honeybees. Estimates were that some commercial beekeepers had lost between thirty and ninety percent of their honeybee colonies. That's a huge range, but even losing thirty percent of these hard-working pollinators could be destructive for farms and, later, for people. Reports were also coming in from Germany, Spain, Greece, and other countries that beekeepers were losing hives.

The buzz about honeybees was that the bees were dying.

This case sounded more serious all the time. I started thinking about what the disappearance of the bees might mean. I wondered if there would be any more honey for sale. I wondered how people would be affected by a big decrease in the number of fruits and nuts available. It seemed like those foods would definitely get more expensive. It also seemed that I might not get honey for my morning toast even if I figured out what happened to the bees. What if they were just gone forever?

I spent the next several months researching why the bees had disappeared. I also decided to title my science project "Vanishing Act: The Mystery of the Disappearing Honeybees." My title was a little more interesting than "Colony Collapse Disorder" (CCD), which is what scientists had officially dubbed the phenomenon. Cell phone towers, certain pesticides, and drought were at first all possible culprits for CCD. Eventually all were ruled out.

By the time I presented my science project at the end of the school year, the best theory available was that a virus had caused bees to weaken and, eventually, die. Some bees may have left the hive and then became too weak to pollinate or to return.

I scored a 98 percent on my presentation of "Vanishing Act." The score wasn't perfect, but it was pretty good.

I really scored on the honey, though. Grandpa Ray dropped off some of the best honey I've ever tasted after he saw my presentation. I don't know where he got it, but that's a mystery I won't worry about solving just yet.

States reporting losses
Non-reporting States

The Smart Swarm

Have you ever seen hundreds of ants moving in an orderly line along a sidewalk? How do so many ants find their way to a spill of soda? They have no sergeants, yet they march like trained soldiers, all focused on a single task. Scientists call this ability to work effectively in large groups *swarm intelligence*.

Think about a good sports team. When team members work well as a group, the team has more success than a team that does not work together. Certain animals also have more success when they work in groups. These animals rely on the work of the group to carry out a number of tasks, including finding food and avoiding predators.

Weaver or tailor ants make an ant bridge to get to their feeding grounds.

Trail Building

When an ant goes to forage, or find food, it leaves a faint trail of a chemical called a *pheromone* along its path. The pheromone has a scent or taste that other ants recognize. When other ants follow the path, they also leave a scented trail. Then the path most traveled becomes the path that is paved with the most pheromone. It is the trail that is easiest to follow and it tends to be the best route to the best food, thanks to the work of the group.

Evasive Moves

When a flock of birds or a school of fish darts away from a predator, it is using the skills of the group to keep it safe. If an individual separates from the group, it would be easy prey. But if the group sticks together, the predator has difficulty focusing on an individual to attack. Swarm intelligence works when one member sees a predator and changes direction, then others in the group immediately react and move together to avoid the predator. The action of the group keeps the animals safe.

A school of bluestriped grunt

Learning from Animals

Scientists are looking at ways to apply swarm intelligence to fleets of robots that can choose the best route through a crowded or dangerous area. Business leaders are using swarm intelligence to determine the best delivery routes. Their truck drivers don't leave a trail of chemicals along the road, but they do share the information about the routes with other drivers, and together they choose the best route. The next time you find yourself in a moving crowd, watch how the group chooses the best route. You might find that people are a bit more like ants than you realized.

Flocks of the red-billed quelea, an African bird, often number in the hundreds of thousands.

Bee, I'm Expecting You

By Emily Dickinson

Bee, I'm expecting you!
Was saying yesterday
To somebody you know
That you were due.

The frogs got home last week,
Are settled and at work,
Birds mostly back,
The clover warm and thick.

You'll get my letter by
The seventeenth; reply,
Or better, be with me.

Yours,
  Fly.

Straight Talk

By Nikki Grimes

Look, Bee

Fair is fair.

I don't burst into

Your honeycomb

Willy-nilly

Or interrupt you

While you feed on

Rose and Lily

So leave me alone, drone

Show yourself the door

And don't come

Buzzing round here

Anymore

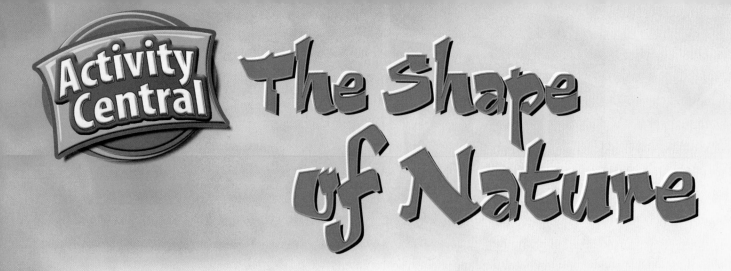

The Shape of Nature

The natural world is filled with patterns. One of these patterns is called a *tessellation*. A tessellation is the repeated pattern of a shape. The sides of the repeated shapes fit together like tiles on a floor.

We can see tessellations in the honeycombs of bees. The repeated shape in the honeycomb is a hexagon, a six-sided figure.

Choose a simple geometric shape and create a tessellation pattern with the shape. Then color each shape and create a mosaic with your tessellation.

Swarming Shapes

Tessellations can also be made with more complex figures. Artists have sometimes used complex tessellation patterns that resemble swarming birds, insects, or fish.

To create your own tessellation pattern of a swarming animal, follow these steps:

1. Cut out a 3-inch by 3-inch square of paper.

2. Draw a line inside the square on one side to represent the head of the animal.

3. Cut along this line, creating two new pieces of paper. Tape the straight edges of these back pieces to the straight edge of the front piece.

4. Draw a line inside the figure on the bottom of the animal to represent a wing or fin.

5. Cut along this line, creating another piece of paper. Tape the straight edge of this wing or fin to the straight edge of the top back piece. Your figure is complete and it should fit with another figure of the same shape.

6. Use this shape to trace a tessellation pattern on a large sheet of paper. Color the shapes similarly so that they resemble a swarm of birds, insects, or fish.

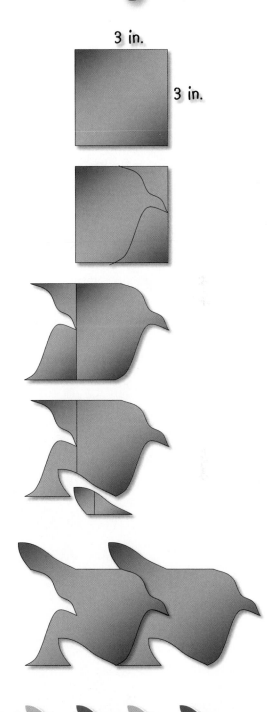

3 in.

3 in.

A Mystery

In "Vanishing Act," Tia tries to solve the mystery of the missing honeybees. She talks to people, gathers information, and considers reasons why the bees are missing. In the end, she doesn't find the bees, but she learns why they may have vanished.

Nature is full of mysteries. Many we have solved, but they still seem mysterious. Why do birds and butterflies migrate? Why do leaves change color? What causes a rainbow? Why are no two snow-flakes alike?

# of Nature

Write a mystery story about something interesting in nature. Think about the weather, animals, plants, or rocks. Even if it's something you know the answer to, have a detective try to solve the mystery by gathering information the way Tia did. Make a story map. Her'es an example to help you write your story.

Story Map

Characters: Jo (girl detective), Dan (friend), Sal (TV meteorologist)	**Setting:** Jo's town

Problem: Why do leaves change color in the fall?

Solution: Less sun causes trees to stop making chlorophyll.

Events:

1. Jo collects leaves for a project.

2. Dan tells her that Jack Frost makes them change color.

3. Jo calls Sal at TV station.

4. He shows her leaf cells under microscope.

ELEPHANTS ON THE SAVANNAH

CAST OF CHARACTERS:
- NARRATOR
- JUDITH: KENYAN RANGER/GUIDE
- MAYA
- ANTONIO
- JORDAN

Narrator: In Kenya, East Africa, it's just before dawn in Amboseli National Park. This famous park is a great place to watch African elephants. Maya, Antonio, and Jordan have traveled here from the United States. Now they are ready for their first day on the savannah.

Judith: Good morning! How was your first night in Amboseli?

Jordan: I'm still tired!

Judith: Don't worry. You'll have a chance to rest after our morning drive. Does everyone have sunscreen and a water bottle?

Maya: It's hard to remember sunscreen when it's still dark out.

Judith: Ready to see African elephants?

Antonio: Definitely! I've got my binoculars.

Judith: This time of day the elephants are usually heading towards the swamps. So we'll go that direction too.

Narrator: Jordan, Maya, and Antonio follow Judith to her jeep and climb in. It gets lighter as they go.

Maya: Wow, there's Mount Kilimanjaro! That is one big mountain.

Antonio: Hey, I see elephants!

Narrator: Eleven elephants are slowly walking near the road. The herd includes two babies. One elephant trumpets loudly.

Jordan: Okay! I'm awake!

Antonio: Wow. That first elephant is one big dude! He must be ten feet tall. And look at those tusks.

Judith: Actually, that "dude" is a female. Herds are family groups led by the oldest female. She is called the matriarch.

Maya: I like that!

Judith: And by the way, African elephants have tusks whether they are male or female.

Jordan: Do the herds always stay together?

Judith: The females and young elephants do. All the females in a herd help teach and protect the calves. They're like "extra moms".

Antonio: Which ones are the dads?

Judith: No dads here. Grown-up males are called bulls. They can weigh six tons or more. Bulls leave their herds when they are about fouteen. After that they live mostly alone.

Antonio: The elephants have stopped walking. It seems like they're listening to something.

Jordan: Want to hear a cool thing I read about elephants?

Maya: I'm all ears.

Jordan: Elephants listen through their feet. Right, Judith?

Judith: Their feet have special vibration sensors. Elephants detect rumbles through the ground. That way they can communicate with other elephants miles away. Elephants make all sorts of other noises. They can scream, grunt, or trumpet. Each sound means something different.

Maya: Antonio, what are you looking at?

Antonio: Check it out. There's another family group way down in the valley. Maybe this herd is talking to that one.

Maya: And now these elephants are walking in that direction. Can we go that way too?

Narrator: the four get in the jeep and head toward the swamp, across open savannah. They park near the elephants.

Maya: Yikes. Aren't we close enough? These are big guys. I mean, big *gals*.

Judith: Don't worry. The females are usually pretty gentle. The ones here in Amboseli are used to jeeps. Let's watch for a while.

Jordan: They sure flap their ears a lot.

Maya: I read about that. The ears have lots of blood veins in them. Flapping cools the blood off in hot weather.

Jordan: Now they're wading in the swamp.

Antonio: Looks like bath time. Look at them spray their own backs with their trunks.

Maya: Those elephants are smart. It's getting hot out here!

Judith: Hey gang, it's almost 9:30. Let's head back to camp. We'll have breakfast. Then later, we can cool off in the camp pool.

Jordan: Yes!

Maya: Sort of like the elephants.

Antonio: Won't we miss some action?

Judith: Not really. During the hottest part of the day, elephants mostly rest in the shade. I want to show you something on the way back.

Narrator: They drive for a few minutes. Judith parks near a pile of big bones.

Jordan: Wow. Did an elephant die here?

Judith: Yes. About two years ago one of the matriarchs died.

Maya: Why are all the bones scattered?

Judith: Elephants mourn their dead. They still stop by here to gently pick up the bones with their trunks. That's why the bones are spread around.

Antonio: I guess they must remember the matriarch.

Judith: They seem to. They also remember people. For example, they will sometimes approach familiar humans, such as researchers they've seen before.

Narrator: The group heads back to camp. Soon, all four are in the pool. The African heat is intense. But by late afternoon it begins to cool off. Shadows become longer as evening approaches.

Judith: Okay, it's four o'clock. Everyone ready to continue our safari?

Maya: Let's go! Do you think we'll get to see elephants eating?

Antonio: I've heard they need at least three hundred pounds of food a day.

Narrator: The four climb back in the jeep. They drive for a few minutes. Then they park in the shade of an acacia tree.

Jordan: There they are. Are those the same elephants we saw before?

Judith: Yes. See the two calves? They are hiding between their mother's legs.

Maya: Did you see that? That elephant picked up a single blade of grass with her trunk! How could she do that?

Judith: There are at least 40,000 muscles in an elephant's trunk. All those muscles mean they can move their trunks very precisely.

Jordan: Those trunks can really multi-task.

Judith: They sure can. Elephants use their trunks to express emotion, eat, smell, drink, touch, make noise, and move things.

Antonio: Check it out. That big elephant is trying to tear out that tree with her trunk. Wow. She did it! She knocked over the whole tree.

Maya: Now she's eating the leaves off the top. So is that calf. How cute.

Jordan: I hear buzzing. Do elephants buzz, too?

Narrator: Suddenly the matriarch begins to run away. The other elephants follow in a hurry.

Judith: Oh no! The trunk of that tree contained a bees' nest! See the bees swarming into that one elephant's eyes?

Antonio: I had no idea elephants could run that fast.

Judith: They can run twenty-four miles per hour. We don't want to get stung either. Let's follow the elephants' lead and get out of here.

Narrator: Everyone piles into the jeep and they zoom away fast.

Maya: Whew. That was close. I'm glad no one was stung.

Jordan: Why is such a big animal afraid of bees?

Antonio: Yeah, isn't their skin too thick to sting through?

Judith: Bees can sting the tender skin behind their ears. Bees can even go up an elephant's trunk.

Jordan: Ouch!

Judith: Let's head back to camp. We'll see more elephants tomorrow. How did you like your first day on the savannah?

Maya: It was fantastic.

Antonio: It sure was! Thank you, Judith.

Jordan: I can't wait to get up tomorrow morning!

A Colossal Catch

Imagine being in a fishing boat when an enormous creature begins to rise from beneath the water! How would you feel? In February 2007, the crew of a New Zealand fishing boat was fishing in the Ross Sea near Antarctica when one of the giants of the deep came to the surface. It was the rarely seen colossal squid.

A hooked fish in its mouth, the squid was almost dead. Still, it took nine people two hours to haul the huge creature onto the boat.

The crew had caught something special. It was the largest colossal squid ever found. From tentacle tip to fin, the squid measured thirty-three feet long and weighed 1,091 pounds. This was an exciting moment for scientists. It was a rare chance to learn more about the colossal squid, believed to be the largest squid in the world.

Mysterious and Frightening

People have long found large squid frightening. For years, sailors told terrifying tales of sea monsters with tangles of arms attacking ships. In Jules Verne's *Twenty Thousand Leagues Under the Sea*, first published in 1870, a ferocious large squid strikes Captain Nemo's submarine. Could these stories have any truth in them? People knew so little about large squid that they weren't sure.

Scientists first identified the colossal squid in 1925 from two arms found in a sperm whale's stomach. Since then, colossal squid have been seen only a few times, and no one has ever studied one in its habitat. These squid live in the icy waters around Antarctica at a depth of more than 3,280 feet. The waters are so dark that it is difficult for scientists to explore.

For years scientists were unable to verify any facts about the colossal squid because there was so little information about it. Most scientists now believe the colossal squid reaches lengths of up to forty-six feet. That's as long as a city bus!

Squid have large eyes for the size of their bodies. The eyes of the colossal squid, as big as dinner plates, are believed to be the largest eyes of any animal. Can you imagine looking into the eye of a colossal squid? Its large eyes help it see prey in the dark ocean depths.

Part of a twenty-foot squid tentacle found off the coast of Japan

A twenty-four foot giant squid, nearly as large as its colossal cousin, attacks a bait squid south of Tokyo, Japan.

The colossal squid is one of the most frightening predators in the ocean. Like other squid, it has eight arms and two longer tentacles. Two rows of sharp, swiveling hooks line the ends of the tentacles. The squid uses these hooks to snag prey.

Awaiting Answers

Today, the colossal squid caught in 2007 is at the Museum of New Zealand in Wellington. It is frozen, but it will be thawed and studied. Scientists want to know many things. How large do colossal squid get? How long do they live? How do they reproduce? Perhaps these and other questions will soon be answered.

The Elephant

By Hilaire Belloc

When people call this beast to mind,
They marvel more and more
At such a little tail behind,
So *large* a trunk before.

By Barbara Juster Esbensen

An evenly balanced
word **WHALE**
it floats
lazily on the page
or dives straight down
to the bottom and beyond
all breath held   held
held   then whoooosh!
The   A   blows its top
into the sun! **WHALE**
serene
sings to us   wet
green sounds from the deepest
part of the alphabet

Comic Creativity

Writers of comic strips and graphic novels use both pictures and words to tell a story. The pictures help show the setting, action, and emotions of the characters.

This week you read stories about two enormous animals—the elephant and the colossal squid. Create a comic strip that features these animals, or two other animals of your choice. Use both pictures and words to tell a story in four to eight panels.

As you create your comic strip, remember these tips:

1. Keep your story simple.

2. Give your story a beginning, middle, and end.

3. Use exact details.

4. Exaggerate the characteristics of your characters to make them humorous.

True or False?

Read the four bizarre animal stories below. Pick the story that just happens to be false. The other three are strange but true.

1 Scientists were thrilled to discover a plump, **purple frog** in western India. The colorful amphibian gives them clues about a frog ancestor that lived 130 million years ago. One scientist called the purple frog "a once-in-a-century find." **TRUE OR FALSE?**

2 A creature called a **sea squirt** is famous for eating its own brain. It uses its simple brain only to find a place to settle for life. Once the sea squirt has found a home, it no longer needs its brain, so it eats it! **TRUE OR FALSE?**

3 A young amphibian called a **walking stick** can stroll on land before it grows legs, as long as it has a willing part-ner. The two amphibians twist together right below their heads. Then they use their snake-shaped bodies as legs to walk along sandy shores. **TRUE OR FALSE?**

4 An **African elephant** has been found imitating traffic noises. A scientist in Kenya noticed a young, orphaned elephant making odd sounds after sunset. It turns out the elephant was imitating the sounds of trucks going down the highway. **TRUE OR FALSE?**

Answer key: 1. true; 2. true; 3. false; 4. true

SPEAKING UP
FOR THE ANIMALS

In "Elephants on the Savannah" and "A Colossal Catch" you read about two of earth's amazing creatures. Harmful human activities have endangered many others.

Think about an animal that you would like to see protected. It can be as big as a blue whale or as small as a monarch butterfly. It can be as exotic as a Siberian tiger or as American as a bald eagle. It can be a mammal or bird; reptile or amphibian; fish or insect. It should be an animal you like and feel strongly about.

Got your animal? Now write a persuasive speech to convince others to protect this animal and its habitat.

SPEECH POINTERS

1. Start your speech by telling why the animal you chose is special. Use interesting facts or tell a personal story about it.

2. Describe problems that this animal faces, such as loss of habitat or the danger of hunters.

3. Explain why you think it is important to protect this animal.

4. Suggest solutions to the problems this animal faces.

5. State how you want listeners to help.

Storm Chasers

Outside, a long siren sounds. On the radio, an announcer says: *"The National Weather Service reports a tornado moving east of Johnstown at 40 mph."*

If we heard a warning like this, most of us would do what we're supposed to do. We would head for shelter indoors. We would retreat to the basement, or to an interior hallway or room such as a closet, staying away from windows. We would use blankets or pillows to cover our bodies and wait for the storm to pass.

But a small group of scientists and researchers would head in the opposite direction—right toward the storm. These people, known as *storm chasers*, pursue tornadoes in specially equipped cars, vans, and trucks. They hope to arrive in time for the worst of the weather, so that they can collect as much information about the storm as possible.

Other storm trackers stay closer to home. These trained volunteers, known as *storm spotters*, keep a close watch on the weather in their own community. They pass along storm information to local weather agencies. Sometimes even sophisticated radar devices don't pick up storms, and the trained eye of the storm spotters can help to save lives. Listen closely to weather reports on your local TV stations and you may hear the forecasters talk about reports they receive from storm spotters.

Tornadoes can strike at any time of year in the United States, but they are generally most common from late winter through mid-summer.

Tornados, like this one near Gruver, Texas, usually form in a large area of the U.S. called Tornado Alley, located between the Rocky Mountains and the Appalachian Mountains.

▲ A hurricane seen from space.

A Hercules weather airplane gets ready. ▶

Both the U.S. Air Force and the National Oceanic and Atmospheric Administration (NOAA) fly missions into storms over the ocean waters.

Hurricane Hunters

Storm chasers don't just follow tornadoes. *Hurricane hunters* take special training to fly planes right into the center of hurricanes and other severe tropical storms.

Outside, heavy rain and high winds batter the aircraft. Inside, the noise is deafening. Despite the roar and the roller coaster ride, the crew carefully collects information on temperature, air pressure, wind speed, and wind direction. This information will be used to help predict the size, strength, and path of the storm.

After flying through the solid ring of thunderstorms that make up the wall of the hurricane, the plane enters a place of near-silence—the eye of the hurricane. Sometimes in this calm center, the hurricane hunters see blue sky, sun, and even stars. But the plane still has to go back through the menacing storm before returning home. In fact, most hurricane hunters make at least four trips through the storm before returning to land!

The hurricane season runs from about June through November in the Pacific and Atlantic oceans.

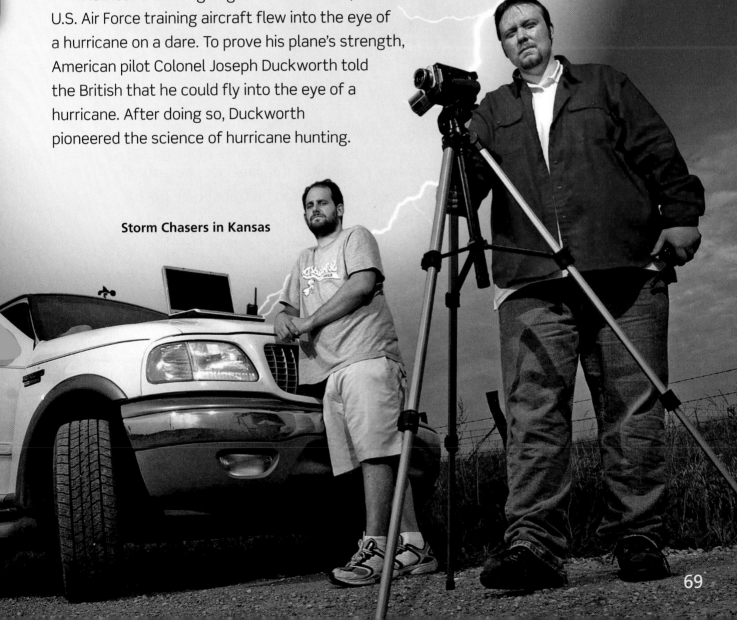

Pioneers of Storm Chasing

Roger Jensen, a North Dakotan, is believed to have been the first storm chaser. "I was born loving storms," he once said. Jensen began chasing storms in 1953 and continued to do so for the next forty years. During his lifetime he took thousands of pictures of storms.

A scientist named Howard Bluestein had an early introduction to storms. In 1954, when Bluestein was five, a hurricane blew the shingles off the roof of his family's house. When he grew up he decided to make storm study his life's work. Today, Bluestein studies storms as a researcher and professor of meteorology at University of Oklahoma. The movie *Twister* was inspired in part by Bluestein's work.

Hurricane hunting began in World War II, when a U.S. Air Force training aircraft flew into the eye of a hurricane on a dare. To prove his plane's strength, American pilot Colonel Joseph Duckworth told the British that he could fly into the eye of a hurricane. After doing so, Duckworth pioneered the science of hurricane hunting.

Storm Chasers in Kansas

Hail, Lightning, Winds, and . . . Traffic Accidents?

Being in a severe storm is dangerous. Storm chasers can be struck by flying debris or by baseball-sized hail. They can be trapped by flash floods or downed power lines. Fortunately, most professional storm chasers keep a safe distance from the deadly storm center—usually one to two miles. They respect the power of the storm.

Lightning is also a great risk to storm chasers. Lightning strikes injure scores of people each year. The risk rises for storm chasers, who spend more time than the average person in the most extreme weather that Mother Nature serves up.

But the riskiest part of storm chasing is actually driving to the storm. Crashes happen because drivers are hurrying to reach the heart of the storm and are looking at the sky instead of the road ahead of them. Blowing dust, heavy rain and fog, hail, skidding on wet pavement, running out of gas, and getting stuck in mud can also make the chase difficult and dangerous.

Hurricane hunters face a different set of risks because they are flying an airplane through the most powerful part of a storm. Violent winds can shake the plane severely, making it difficult to fly. Equipment inside the plane can get tossed around, causing possible injury. The wind can also damage the aircraft, and a sudden blast can send a plane plunging into the ocean.

Storm spotting and storm chasing should never be done without proper training, experience, and equipment. Hurricane hunting is an activity for experts. For most of us, the best way to experience storm chasing is by watching a TV documentary or movie! As long as there are storm chasers filming the most dramatic weather events, we can sit in the safety of our homes and movie theaters and comfortably experience nature at its wildest.

WHITEOUT!
The Great Blizzard of 1888

A Slow Start

On March 10, the weather up and down the East Coast was clear and unseasonably warm. It was so pleasant that people headed outdoors to enjoy the warm temperatures. Some families even went picnicking. But while spring appeared to be knocking on the door, winter wasn't over.

The blizzard that was later nicknamed "The Great White Hurricane" began as a drizzle on March 11. The rain grew heavier overnight and quickly changed to snow as temperatures fell below zero. A ferocious wind developed.

People in small towns and big cities from Maryland to Maine woke up the next morning to heavy snowfall. Surely they were surprised by the sudden change in the weather, but many went about their lives as usual.

Farmers braved howling winds to tend to their animals. Children trudged to school. Workers sloshed their way to their jobs. Among those who braved the blizzard in New York City was future president Theodore Roosevelt. He slogged through the snow to keep an appointment with a librarian, only to find she had stayed home.

A New York City street during the Blizzard of 1888. Many power lines were brought down by the snow and high winds.

A grocery awning has collapsed under the weight of the snow. Drifts up to fifty feet deep were reported.

Buried Under Snow

By noon on March 12, many areas in the Northeast were already buried under a blanket of snow. In some places, huge snow-drifts covered trees and the tops of houses. Families were trapped in their homes without food or fuel, hungry and cold. Trains were stopped in their tracks. Fire stations couldn't mobilize to fight fires. Communication became impossible when telegraph and telephone lines snapped under the weight of the snow. High winds helped to ground or wreck more than two hundred ships.

But the blizzard wasn't finished. For thirty-six hours, snow continued to fall. When it finally did stop, the blizzard had dumped between forty and fifty inches of snow in Connecticut, Maine, Massachusetts, New York, and New Jersey. It took weeks for people to completely dig out. In all, hundreds died from the storm and the cold. The Great Blizzard of 1888 has taken its place in history as America's most famous snowstorm.

Weather

Whether the weather be fine,
Or whether the weather be not,
Whether the weather be cold,
Or whether the weather be hot,
We'll weather the weather
Whatever the weather
Whether we like it or not.

Anonymous

In the Night

In the night
The rain comes down.
Yonder at the edge of the earth
There is a sound of cracking,
There is a sound of falling.
Down yonder it goes on slowly rumbling,
It goes on shaking.

from *Papago Indians*

Snow

The word begins to melt
inside my pocket. SNOW.
I fling its lacy coldness
in the air, then watch it
floating there.

Nikki Grimes

The Wind

The morning after the night before,
   The wind came in when I opened the door.
It blew the "Welcome" off the mat.
   It blew the fur right off my cat.
It blew my shirttail out of my pants.
   It grabbed the curtains and started to dance
Around and around and around about
   Till I opened a window and kicked it out.

John Ciardi

Weather in a Box

Blizzard Blaster

Create your own blizzard!

**Need a day off from school?
Is summer making you sweat?
Open the box!**

Winter, spring, summer, or fall—let it snow!

I magine that you work for a company that makes weather you can carry in a box. Create a poster advertising your product. You can choose any kind of weather—blizzard, fog, rain, sunshine, even a tornado.

Include artwork and give your product a catchy name and slogan. Your poster should include the following information:

※ Who the target audience is
※ Why people should buy this product
※ How people can use it

Capture It with a Caption

Suppose you are a writer and photographer for a newspaper. Your job is to take pictures and to write captions for them—short descriptions that tell about the pictures in one or two sentences.

Study the pictures on this page and read the information about them. Then write captions that capture, or vividly describe, what each picture is about.

- What: Dust Storm
- Where: Stratford, Texas
- When: April 18, 1935

- What: Lightning
- Where: Nanjing, China
- When: August 1, 2006

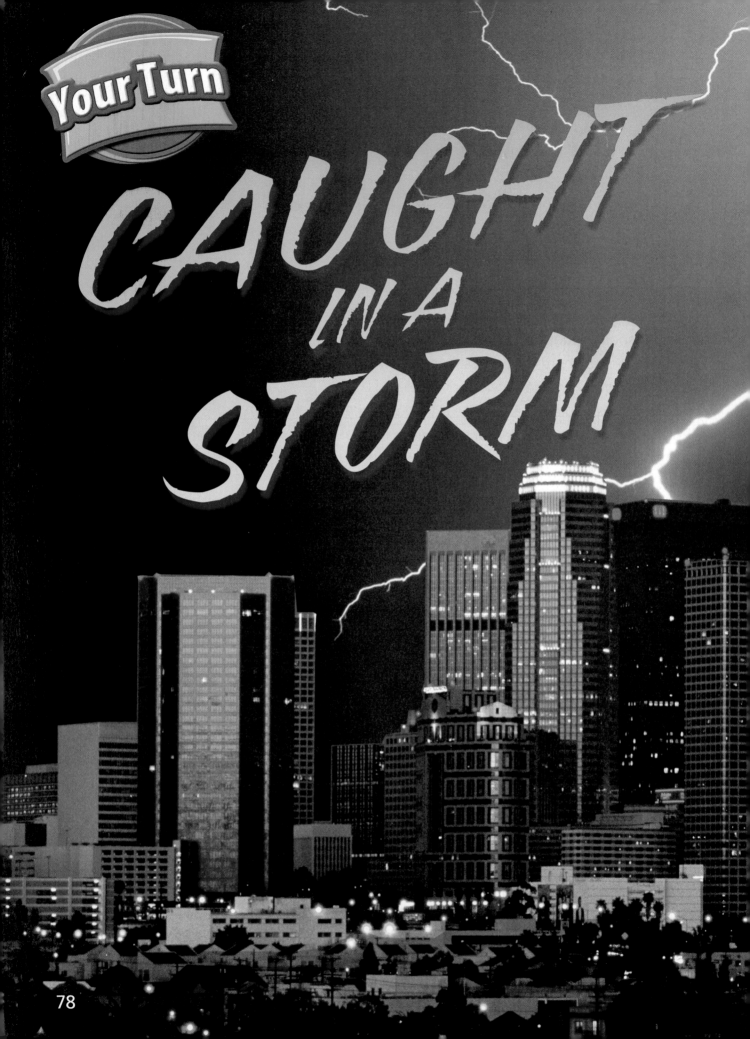

CAUGHT IN A STORM

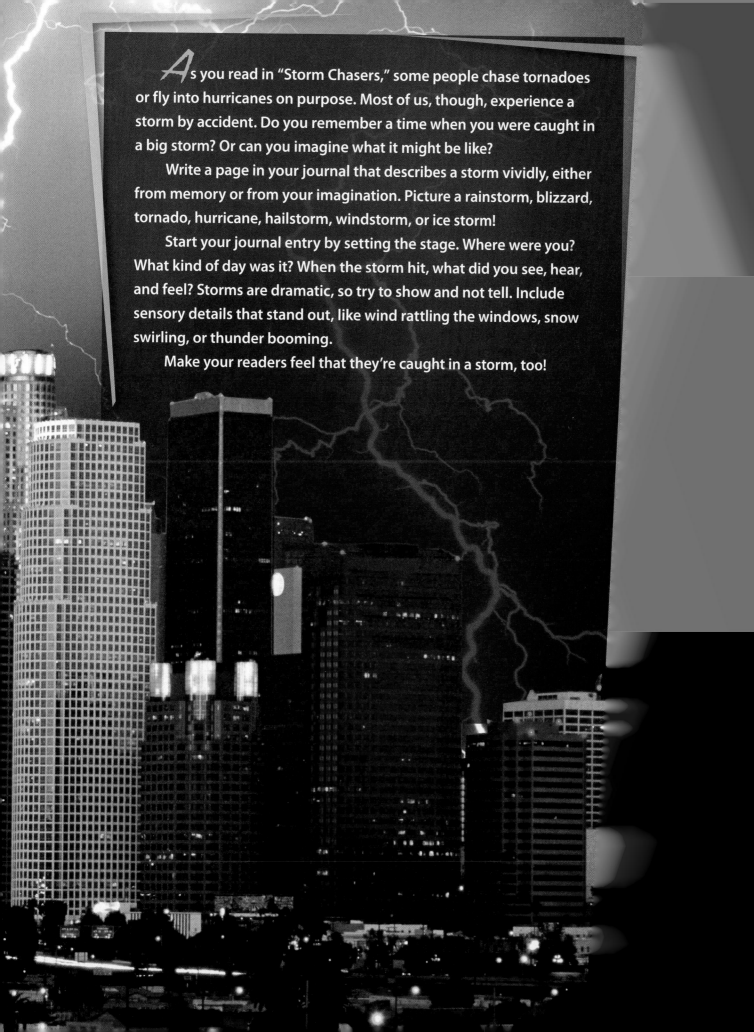

As you read in "Storm Chasers," some people chase tornadoes or fly into hurricanes on purpose. Most of us, though, experience a storm by accident. Do you remember a time when you were caught in a big storm? Or can you imagine what it might be like?

Write a page in your journal that describes a storm vividly, either from memory or from your imagination. Picture a rainstorm, blizzard, tornado, hurricane, hailstorm, windstorm, or ice storm!

Start your journal entry by setting the stage. Where were you? What kind of day was it? When the storm hit, what did you see, hear, and feel? Storms are dramatic, so try to show and not tell. Include sensory details that stand out, like wind rattling the windows, snow swirling, or thunder booming.

Make your readers feel that they're caught in a storm, too!

California Standards

English-Language Arts Content Standards

Page where standards are found:

Reading

WORD ANALYSIS, FLUENCY, AND SYSTEMIC VOCABULARY DEVELOPMENT

R1.0 Students use their knowledge of word origins and word relationships, as well as historical and literary context clues, to determine the meaning of specialized vocabulary and to understand the precise meaning of grade-level-appropriate words.

Word Recognition

R1.1 Read aloud narrative and expository text fluently and accurately and with appropriate pacing, intonation, and expression.

Vocabulary and Concept Development

R1.2 Use word origins to determine the meaning of unknown words.

R1.3 Understand and explain frequently used synonyms, antonyms, and homographs.

R1.4 Know abstract, derived roots and affixes from Greek and Latin and use this knowledge to analyze the meaning of complex words (e.g., *controversial*).

R1.5 Understand and explain the figurative and metaphorical use of words in context.

READING COMPREHENSION (FOCUS ON INFORMATIONAL MATERIALS)

R2.0 Students read and understand grade-level-appropriate material. They describe and connect the essential ideas, arguments, and perspectives of the text by using their knowledge of text structure, organization, and purpose.

Structural Features of Informational Materials

R2.1 Understand how text features (e.g., format, graphics, sequence, diagrams, illustrations, charts, maps) make information accessible and usable.

R2.2 Analyze text that is organized in sequential or chronological order.

Comprehension and Analysis of Grade-Level-Appropriate Text

R2.3 Discern main ideas and concepts presented in texts, identifying and assessing evidence that supports those ideas.

R2.4 Draw inferences, conclusions, or generalizations about text and support them with textual evidence and prior knowledge.

Expository Critique

R2.5 Distinguish facts, supported inferences, and opinions in text.

LITERARY RESPONSE AND ANALYSIS

R3.0 Students read and respond to historically or culturally significant works of literature. They begin to find ways to clarify the ideas and make connections between literary works.

Structural Features of Literature

R3.1 Identify and analyze the characteristics of poetry, drama, fiction, and nonfiction and explain the appropriateness of the literary forms chosen by an author for a specific purpose.

Narrative Analysis of Grade-Level-Appropriate Text

R3.2 Identify the main problem or conflict of the plot and explain how it is resolved.

R3.3 Contrast the actions, motives (e.g., loyalty, selfishness, conscientiousness), and appearances of characters in a work of fiction and discuss the importance of the contrasts to the plot or theme.

R3.4 Understand that theme refers to the meaning or moral of a selection and recognize themes (whether implied or stated directly) in sample works.

R3.5 Describe the function and effect of common literary devices (e.g., imagery, metaphor, symbolism).

R3.3 Analyze the influence of setting on the problem and its resolution.

R3.4 Define how tone or meaning is conveyed in poetry through word choice, figurative language, sentence structure, line length, punctuation, rhythm, repetition, and rhyme.

R3.5 Identify the speaker and recognize the difference between first- and third-person narration (e.g., autobiography compared with biography).

R3.6 Identify and analyze features of themes conveyed through characters, actions, and images.

R3.7 Explain the effects of common literary devices (e.g., symbolism, imagery, metaphor) in a variety of fictional and nonfictional texts.

Literary Criticism

R3.8 Critique the credibility of characterization and the degree to which a plot is contrived or realistic (e.g., compare use of fact and fantasy in historical fiction).

Writing

WRITING STRATEGIES

W1.0 Students write clear, coherent, and focused essays. The writing exhibits students' awareness of the audience and purpose. Essays contain formal introductions, supporting evidence, and conclusions. Students progress through the stages of the writing process as needed.

Organization and Focus

W1.1 Choose the form of writing (e.g., personal letter, letter to the editor, review, poem, report, narrative) that best suits the intended purpose.

W1.2 Create multiple-paragraph expository compositions:

W1.2.a Engage the interest of the reader and state a clear purpose.

W1.2.b Develop the topic with supporting details and precise verbs, nouns, and adjectives to paint a visual image in the mind of the reader.

W1.2.c Conclude with a detailed summary linked to the purpose of the composition.

W1.3 Use a variety of effective and coherent organizational patterns, including comparison and contrast; organization by categories; and arrangement by spatial order, order of importance, or climactic order.

Research and Technology

W1.4 Use organizational features of electronic text (e.g., bulletin boards, databases, keyword searches, e-mail addresses) to locate information.

W1.5 Compose documents with appropriate formatting by using word-processing skills and principles of design (e.g., margins, tabs, spacing, columns, page orientation).

Evaluation and Revision

W1.6 Revise writing to improve the organization and consistency of ideas within and between paragraphs.

WRITING APPLICATIONS (GENRES AND THEIR CHARACTERISTICS)

W2.0 Students write narrative, expository, persuasive, and descriptive texts of at least 500 to 700 words in each genre.

Using the writing strategies of grade six outlined in Writing Standard 1.0, students:

W2.1 Write narratives:

W2.1.a Establish and develop a plot and setting and present a point of view that is appropriate to the stories.

W2.1.b Include sensory details and concrete language to develop plot and character.

W2.1.c Use a range of narrative devices (e.g., dialogue, suspense).

W2.2 Write expository compositions (e.g., description, explanation, comparison and contrast, problem and solution):

W2.2.a State the thesis or purpose.

W2.2.b Explain the situation.

W2.2.c Follow an organizational pattern appropriate to the type of composition.

W2.2.d Offer persuasive evidence to validate arguments and conclusions as needed.

W2.3 Write research reports:

W2.3.a Pose relevant questions with a scope narrow enough to be thoroughly covered.

W2.3.b Support the main idea or ideas with facts, details, examples, and explanations from multiple authoritative sources (e.g., speakers, periodicals, online information searches).

W2.3.c Include a bibliography.

W2.4 Write responses to literature:

W2.4.a Develop an interpretation exhibiting careful reading, understanding, and insight.

W2.4.b Organize the interpretation around several clear ideas, premises, or images.

W2.4.c Develop and justify the interpretation through sustained use of examples and textual evidence.

W2.5 Write persuasive compositions:

W2.5.a State a clear position on a proposition or proposal.

W2.5.b Support the position with organized and relevant evidence.

W2.5.c Anticipate and address reader concerns and counterarguments.

Written and Oral English Language Conventions

WRITTEN AND ORAL ENGLISH LANGUAGE CONVENTIONS

LC1.0 Students write and speak with a command of standard English conventions appropriate to this grade level.

Sentence Structure

LC1.1 Use simple, compound, and compound-complex sentences; use effective coordination and subordination of ideas to express complete thoughts.

Grammar

LC1.2 Identify and properly use indefinite pronouns and present perfect, past perfect, and future perfect verb tenses; ensure that verbs agree with compound subjects.

Punctuation

LC1.3 Use colons after the salutation in business letters, semicolons to connect independent clauses, and commas when linking two clauses with a conjunction in compound sentences.

Capitalization

LC1.4 Use correct capitalization.

Spelling

LC1.5 Spell frequently misspelled words correctly (e.g., *their, they're, there*).

Listening and Speaking

LISTENING AND SPEAKING STRATEGIES

LS1.0 Students deliver focused, coherent presentations that convey ideas clearly and relate to the background and interests of the audience. They evaluate the content of oral communication.

Comprehension

LS1.1 Relate the speaker's verbal communication (e.g., word choice, pitch, feeling, tone) to the nonverbal message (e.g., posture, gesture).

LS1.2 Identify the tone, mood, and emotion conveyed in the oral communication.

LS1.3 Restate and execute multiple-step oral instructions and directions.

Organization and Delivery of Oral Communication

LS1.4 Select a focus, an organizational structure, and a point of view, matching the purpose, message, occasion, and vocal modulation to the audience.

LS1.5 Emphasize salient points to assist the listener in following the main ideas and concepts.

LS1.6 Support opinions with detailed evidence and with visual or media displays that use appropriate technology.

LS1.7 Use effective rate, volume, pitch, and tone and align nonverbal elements to sustain audience interest and attention.

Analysis and Evaluation of Oral and Media Communications

LS1.8 Analyze the use of rhetorical devices (e.g., cadence, repetitive patterns, use of onomatopoeia) for intent and effect.

LS1.9 Identify persuasive and propaganda techniques used in television and identify false and misleading information.

SPEAKING APPLICATIONS (GENRES AND THEIR CHARACTERISTICS)

LS2.0 Students deliver well-organized formal presentations employing traditional rhetorical strategies (e.g., narration, exposition, persuasion, description).

Using the speaking strategies of grade six outlined in Listening and Speaking Standard 1.0, students:

LS2.1 Deliver narrative presentations:

LS2.1.a Establish a context, plot, and point of view.

LS2.1.b Include sensory details and concrete language to develop the plot and character.

LS2.1.c Use a range of narrative devices (e.g., dialogue, tension, or suspense).

LS2.2 Deliver informative presentations:

LS2.2.a Pose relevant questions sufficiently limited in scope to be completely and thoroughly answered.

LS2.2.b Develop the topic with facts, details, examples, and explanations from multiple authoritative sources (e.g., speakers, periodicals, online information).

LS2.3 Deliver oral responses to literature:

LS2.3.a Develop an interpretation exhibiting careful reading, understanding, and insight.

LS2.3.b Organize the selected interpretation around several clear ideas, premises, or images.

LS2.3.c Develop and justify the selected interpretation through sustained use of examples and textual evidence.

LS2.4 Deliver persuasive presentations:

LS2.4.a Provide a clear statement of the position.

LS2.4.b Include relevant evidence.

LS2.4.c Offer a logical sequence of information.

LS2.4.d Engage the listener and foster acceptance of the proposition or proposal.

LS2.5 Deliver presentations on problems and solutions:

LS2.5.a Theorize on the causes and effects of each problem and establish connections between the defined problem and at least one solution.

LS2.6 Offer persuasive evidence to validate the definition of the problem and the proposed solutions.

Photography Credits:

Cover (bkgd) © Jim Reed /Getty Images, **(t)** © AP Photo, **(b)** © Don Farral/Getty Images; **Opener (t)** © Paul Chesley/National Geographic Image Collection, **(b)** © Art Wolfe/Getty Images; **1 (br)** © NASA/Photo Researchers, Inc., **(can)** © Detlev van Ravenswaay/Photo Researchers, Inc., **(flame)** © Don Farrall/Getty Images, **(bl)** © James Stevenson/Dorling Kindersley; **2 (c)** © Gavin Hellier/ Jon Arnold Images Ltd /Alamy, **(t)** © AP Photo/Anchorage Daily News, Melodie Wright, **(b)** © Thomas Fricke/Corbis; **3 (c)** © Pat Powers and Cherryl Schafer/Getty Images, **(b)** © Scott Stulberg/Corbis, **(t)** © Art Wolfe/Getty Images; **4, 5, 7, 8 (can)** © Detlev van Ravensuaay/Photo Researchers, Inc.; **4–7 (bkgd)** Stockbyte/Getty Images; **5, 7, 8 (flame)** © Don Farrall/Getty Images; **6** © David Ducros/Photo Researchers, Inc.; **7 (b)** © Detlev van Ravensuaay/Photo Researchers, Inc.; **8 (r)** © Julian Baum/Photo Researchers, Inc.; **9 (b)** © NASA; **10** © Stocktrek Images/Getty Images; **12** © RF Corbis; **13** © NASA; **14** © Corbis; **16 (t)** © James Stevenson/Dorling Kindersley, **(b)** © NASA/Photo Researchers, Inc.; **18** © Jeff Schultz/ photolibrary.com; **18–25 (bkgd)** © Dorling Kindersley/Getty Images; **19** © WorldFoto/Alamy; **20** © William W. Bacon III/Photo Researchers, Inc.; **21** © Don Mason/Corbis; **22** © Brett Baunton/Alamy; **23** © blickwinkel/Alamy; **24 (tr)** © Danita Delimont/Alamy, **(bl)** © AP Photo/ Anchorage Daily News, Melodie Wright; **25 (t)** © Siede Preis/Getty Images, **(b)** © NPS; **26 (t)** © Paul Chesley/National Geographic Image Collection, **(b)** © Phil Schermeister/National Geographic Image Collection; **26–27 (border)** © Don Farrall/Getty Images; **27 (t)** © Gary Corbett/ Alamy; **28** © Paul van Gaalen/zefa/Corbis; **29** © Kazuyoshi Nomachi/Corbis Algeria; **30 (t)** © Imagemore Co., Ltd./Getty Images, **(b)** © Martin Rogers/Workbook Stock/Jupiter Images; **31** © Alaska Stock LLC/Alamy; **32 (br)** © Jack Jackson/ Robert Harding Picture Library Ltd/Alamy, **(bl)** © Gavin Hellier/Jon Arnold Images Ltd/Alamy; **32–33 (bkgd)** © Siede Preis/Getty Images; **33 (l)** © Steve Allen/ The Image Bank/Getty Images, **(r)** © Caroline Schiff/Photographer's Choice/Getty Images; **34–41 (bee)** © Don Farral /Getty Images; **36** © Thomas Fricke/Corbis; **37** © Martin Jepp/zefa/Corbis; **38** © Scot Frei/Corbis; **39** © Joe Drivas/Getty Images; **40** © Carmen Redondo/Corbis; **42 (bl)** © Hornbil Images/Alamy; **42–43 (bkgd)** © Siede Preis/Photodisc/Getty; **42, 43 (ants)** © Burke/Triolo Productions/Brand X/Corbis; **43 (t)** © Birgitte Wilms/Getty Images, **(b)** © Peter Johnson/Corbis; **46 (c)** © Image Source/Corbis, **(bkgd)** © PhotoDisc, Inc./Getty Images; **47** © PhotoDisc, Inc./Getty Images; **48 (bl)** © Edmond Van Hoorick/Getty Images, **(br)** © Gerben Oppermans/Getty Images; **48–49 (leaves)** © Steve Cole/Photodisc, Inc./Getty Images; **50–57** Edmond Van Hoorick/Getty Images, **(b)** © Art Wolfe/Getty Images; **52** © Joseph Van Os/Getty Images; **53** © maggiegowan.co.uk/ Alamy; **54** © Paul Souders/Corbis; **55** © Werner Bollmann/Getty Images; **56** © Panoramic Images/Getty Images; **57** © Beverly Joubert/National Geographic Image Collection; **59 (t)** © AP Photo/HO, National Science Museum, **(b)** © AP Photo/Tsunemi Kubodera of the National Science Museum of Japan, HO; **60 (bkgd)** © Ryan McVay/Getty Images, **(c)** © D. Allen Photography/Animals Animals – Earth Scenes – All rights reserved.; **61** © Gerard Lacz/Animals Animals – Earth Scenes – All rights reserved.; **62, 63 (bkgd)** © Photodisc, Inc/Getty Images; **63 (corners)** © Ian Cartwright/Getty Images; **64 (l)** © Keren Su, **(r)** © Pat Powers and Cherryl Schafer/Getty Images; **64–65 (bkgd)** © Alan and Sandy Carey/Getty Images; **65 (l)** © PhotoLink/Getty Images; **65 (r)** © Kim Steele/Getty Images; **66–67 (bkgd)** © John Hone/africanpictures. net/The Image Works; **66–67 (t)** © PhotoDisc, Inc./Getty Images; **67 (t)** © Robert Glusic/Getty Images, **(b)** © A. T. Willett/Alamy; **68 (tl)** © Photodisc /SuperStock, **(tr)** © Photo Researchers, Inc.; **69** © AP Photo/The Morning Sun, Andrew D. Brosig; **70** © Eric Nguyen/Corbis; **71** © Carsten Peter/National Geographic Image Collection; **72, 73** © AP Photo; **76 (l)** © Jim West/The Image Works, **(bkgd)** © PhotoLink/Getty Images; **77 (t)** © PhotoSpin, Inc /Alamy, **(br)** © AP Photos, **(bl)** © NOAA George E. Marsh Album; **78–79** © Scott Stulberg/Corbis.

Illustration Credits:

5 Anthology, Inc.; **10, 11** Jennifer Hewitson; **14** Dave Klug; **15** Stephen Costanza; **17** Ben Shannon; **34 (t)** Michael Chesworth; **34–41 (bkgd)** Anthology, Inc.; **41** Susan Carlson; **44–45** Jon Goodell; **46, 47** Anthology, Inc.; **62** Brian White; **74, 75** Sally Wern Comport